This Recipe Book Belongs To:

Table of Contents

Recipe   Page No

Table of Contents

Recipe   Page No

Table of Contents

Recipe   Page No

Bowes Publishing

Recipe

Source

Serves   Prep time   Cook time

My Rating   ☆ ☆ ☆   ☆ ☆

Difficulty   ☆ ☆ ☆   ☆ ☆

Vegan ☐   Gluten Free ☐   Low FODMAP ☐

Vegetarian ☐   Diary Free ☐   Low Carb ☐

Ingredients

Additional Notes

Method

Recipe _____

Source _____

Serves _____   Prep time _____   Cook time _____

My Rating   ☆ ☆ ☆ ☆ ☆

Difficulty   ☆ ☆ ☆ ☆ ☆

Vegan ☐   Gluten Free ☐   Low FODMAP ☐

Vegetarian ☐   Diary Free ☐   Low Carb ☐

Ingredients

_____
_____
_____
_____
_____
_____

Additional Notes

_____
_____
_____
_____

Method

Recipe _____

Source _____

Serves _____ Prep time _____ Cook time _____

My Rating ☆ ☆ ☆ ☆ ☆

Difficulty ☆ ☆ ☆ ☆ ☆

Vegan ☐   Gluten Free ☐   Low FODMAP ☐

Vegetarian ☐   Diary Free ☐   Low Carb ☐

Ingredients

_____

_____

_____

_____

_____

_____

Additional Notes

_____

_____

_____

_____

_____

Method

Recipe

Source

Serves   Prep time   Cook time

My Rating   ☆ ☆ ☆ ☆ ☆

Difficulty   ☆ ☆ ☆ ☆ ☆

Vegan ☐   Gluten Free ☐   Low FODMAP ☐

Vegetarian ☐   Diary Free ☐   Low Carb ☐

Ingredients

Additional Notes

Method

Recipe _____

Source _____

Serves _____   Prep time _____   Cook time _____

My Rating ☆ ☆ ☆ ☆ ☆

Difficulty ☆ ☆ ☆ ☆ ☆

Vegan ☐   Gluten Free ☐   Low FODMAP ☐

Vegetarian ☐   Diary Free ☐   Low Carb ☐

Ingredients

_____
_____
_____
_____
_____
_____

Additional Notes

_____
_____
_____
_____

Method

Recipe _____

Source _____

| Serves _____ | Prep time _____ | Cook time _____ |

My Rating ☆ ☆ ☆ ☆ ☆

Difficulty ☆ ☆ ☆ ☆ ☆

Vegan ☐   Gluten Free ☐   Low FODMAP ☐

Vegetarian ☐   Diary Free ☐   Low Carb ☐

Ingredients

_____

_____

_____

_____

_____

_____

Additional Notes

_____

_____

_____

_____

_____

Method

Recipe _____

Source _____

Serves _____ Prep time _____ Cook time _____

My Rating ☆ ☆ ☆ ☆ ☆

Difficulty ☆ ☆ ☆ ☆ ☆

Vegan ☐ Gluten Free ☐ Low FODMAP ☐

Vegetarian ☐ Diary Free ☐ Low Carb ☐

Ingredients

_____

_____

_____

_____

_____

Additional Notes

_____

_____

_____

_____

Method

Recipe _____

Source _____

Serves _____ Prep time _____ Cook time _____

My Rating ☆ ☆ ☆ ☆ ☆

Difficulty ☆ ☆ ☆ ☆ ☆

Vegan ☐   Gluten Free ☐   Low FODMAP ☐

Vegetarian ☐   Diary Free ☐   Low Carb ☐

Ingredients

_____

_____

_____

_____

_____

_____

Additional Notes

_____

_____

_____

_____

Method

Recipe
Source

Serves   Prep time   Cook time

My Rating   ☆   ☆   ☆   ☆   ☆

Difficulty   ☆   ☆   ☆   ☆   ☆

Vegan ☐   Gluten Free ☐   Low FODMAP ☐

Vegetarian ☐   Diary Free ☐   Low Carb ☐

Ingredients

Additional Notes

Method

Recipe

Source

Serves   Prep time   Cook time

My Rating   ☆ ☆ ☆ ☆ ☆

Difficulty   ☆ ☆ ☆ ☆ ☆

Vegan ☐   Gluten Free ☐   Low FODMAP ☐

Vegetarian ☐   Diary Free ☐   Low Carb ☐

Ingredients

Additional Notes

Method

Recipe

Source

Serves   Prep time   Cook time

My Rating   ☆   ☆   ☆   ☆   ☆

Difficulty   ☆   ☆   ☆   ☆   ☆

Vegan ☐   Gluten Free ☐   Low FODMAP ☐

Vegetarian ☐   Diary Free ☐   Low Carb ☐

Ingredients

Additional Notes

Method

Recipe

Source

Serves   Prep time   Cook time

My Rating   ☆   ☆   ☆   ☆   ☆

Difficulty   ☆   ☆   ☆   ☆   ☆

Vegan ☐   Gluten Free ☐   Low FODMAP ☐

Vegetarian ☐   Diary Free ☐   Low Carb ☐

Ingredients

Additional Notes

Method

Recipe

Source

Serves   Prep time   Cook time

My Rating   ☆   ☆   ☆   ☆   ☆

Difficulty   ☆   ☆   ☆   ☆   ☆

Vegan ☐   Gluten Free ☐   Low FODMAP ☐

Vegetarian ☐   Diary Free ☐   Low Carb ☐

Ingredients

Additional Notes

Method

Recipe _____

Source _____

Serves _____ Prep time _____ Cook time _____

My Rating ☆ ☆ ☆ ☆ ☆

Difficulty ☆ ☆ ☆ ☆ ☆

Vegan ☐   Gluten Free ☐   Low FODMAP ☐

Vegetarian ☐   Diary Free ☐   Low Carb ☐

Ingredients

_____

_____

_____

_____

_____

_____

Additional Notes

_____

_____

_____

_____

Method

Recipe _____

Source _____

Serves _____ Prep time _____ Cook time _____

My Rating ☆ ☆ ☆ ☆ ☆

Difficulty ☆ ☆ ☆ ☆ ☆

Vegan ☐ Gluten Free ☐ Low FODMAP ☐

Vegetarian ☐ Diary Free ☐ Low Carb ☐

Ingredients

_____

_____

_____

_____

_____

_____

_____

Additional Notes

_____

_____

_____

_____

Method

Recipe _____

Source _____

Serves _____ Prep time _____ Cook time _____

My Rating ☆ ☆ ☆ ☆ ☆

Difficulty ☆ ☆ ☆ ☆ ☆

Vegan ☐   Gluten Free ☐   Low FODMAP ☐

Vegetarian ☐   Diary Free ☐   Low Carb ☐

Ingredients

_____

_____

_____

_____

_____

_____

_____

Additional Notes

_____

_____

_____

_____

Method

Recipe _____

Source _____

Serves _____ Prep time _____ Cook time _____

My Rating ☆ ☆ ☆ ☆ ☆

Difficulty ☆ ☆ ☆ ☆ ☆

Vegan ☐   Gluten Free ☐   Low FODMAP ☐

Vegetarian ☐   Diary Free ☐   Low Carb ☐

Ingredients

_____

_____

_____

_____

_____

_____

Additional Notes

_____

_____

_____

_____

Method

Recipe _____

Source _____

Serves _____ Prep time _____ Cook time _____

My Rating ☆ ☆ ☆ ☆ ☆

Difficulty ☆ ☆ ☆ ☆ ☆

Vegan ☐   Gluten Free ☐   Low FODMAP ☐

Vegetarian ☐   Diary Free ☐   Low Carb ☐

Ingredients

_____
_____
_____
_____
_____
_____
_____

Additional Notes

_____
_____
_____
_____
_____

Method

Recipe _____

Source _____

Serves _____ Prep time _____ Cook time _____

My Rating ☆ ☆ ☆ ☆ ☆

Difficulty ☆ ☆ ☆ ☆ ☆

Vegan ☐   Gluten Free ☐   Low FODMAP ☐

Vegetarian ☐   Diary Free ☐   Low Carb ☐

Ingredients

_____
_____
_____
_____
_____
_____

Additional Notes

_____
_____
_____
_____

Method

Recipe _____

Source _____

Serves _____ Prep time _____ Cook time _____

My Rating ☆ ☆ ☆ ☆ ☆

Difficulty ☆ ☆ ☆ ☆ ☆

Vegan ☐   Gluten Free ☐   Low FODMAP ☐

Vegetarian ☐   Diary Free ☐   Low Carb ☐

Ingredients

_____

_____

_____

_____

_____

_____

Additional Notes

_____

_____

_____

_____

Method

Recipe _____

Source _____

Serves _____ Prep time _____ Cook time _____

My Rating ☆ ☆ ☆ ☆ ☆

Difficulty ☆ ☆ ☆ ☆ ☆

Vegan ☐   Gluten Free ☐   Low FODMAP ☐

Vegetarian ☐   Diary Free ☐   Low Carb ☐

Ingredients

_____
_____
_____
_____
_____
_____

Additional Notes

_____
_____
_____
_____
_____

Method

Recipe _____

Source _____

Serves _____   Prep time _____   Cook time _____

My Rating ☆ ☆ ☆ ☆ ☆

Difficulty ☆ ☆ ☆ ☆ ☆

Vegan ☐   Gluten Free ☐   Low FODMAP ☐

Vegetarian ☐   Diary Free ☐   Low Carb ☐

Ingredients

_____

_____

_____

_____

_____

_____

Additional Notes

_____

_____

_____

_____

_____

Method

Recipe _____

Source _____

Serves _____ Prep time _____ Cook time _____

My Rating ☆ ☆ ☆ ☆ ☆

Difficulty ☆ ☆ ☆ ☆ ☆

Vegan ☐   Gluten Free ☐   Low FODMAP ☐

Vegetarian ☐   Diary Free ☐   Low Carb ☐

Ingredients

_____

_____

_____

_____

_____

_____

Additional Notes

_____

_____

_____

_____

Method

Recipe

Source

Serves   Prep time   Cook time

My Rating   ☆ ☆ ☆   ☆ ☆

Difficulty   ☆ ☆ ☆   ☆ ☆

Vegan ☐   Gluten Free ☐   Low FODMAP ☐

Vegetarian ☐   Diary Free ☐   Low Carb ☐

Ingredients

Additional Notes

Method

Recipe _____

Source _____

Serves _____ Prep time _____ Cook time _____

My Rating ☆ ☆ ☆ ☆ ☆

Difficulty ☆ ☆ ☆ ☆ ☆

Vegan ☐   Gluten Free ☐   Low FODMAP ☐

Vegetarian ☐   Diary Free ☐   Low Carb ☐

Ingredients

_____

_____

_____

_____

_____

_____

Additional Notes

_____

_____

_____

_____

_____

Method

Recipe _____

Source _____

Serves _____ Prep time _____ Cook time _____

My Rating ☆ ☆ ☆ ☆ ☆

Difficulty ☆ ☆ ☆ ☆ ☆

Vegan ☐   Gluten Free ☐   Low FODMAP ☐

Vegetarian ☐   Diary Free ☐   Low Carb ☐

Ingredients

_____

_____

_____

_____

_____

_____

Additional Notes

_____

_____

_____

_____

Method

Recipe _____

Source _____

Serves _____ Prep time _____ Cook time _____

My Rating ☆ ☆ ☆ ☆ ☆

Difficulty ☆ ☆ ☆ ☆ ☆

Vegan ☐   Gluten Free ☐   Low FODMAP ☐

Vegetarian ☐   Diary Free ☐   Low Carb ☐

Ingredients

_____
_____
_____
_____
_____
_____
_____

Additional Notes

_____
_____
_____
_____
_____

Method

Recipe

Source

Serves   Prep time   Cook time

My Rating   ☆   ☆   ☆   ☆   ☆

Difficulty   ☆   ☆   ☆   ☆   ☆

Vegan ☐   Gluten Free ☐   Low FODMAP ☐

Vegetarian ☐   Diary Free ☐   Low Carb ☐

Ingredients

Additional Notes

Method

Recipe _____

Source _____

Serves _____ Prep time _____ Cook time _____

My Rating ☆ ☆ ☆ ☆ ☆

Difficulty ☆ ☆ ☆ ☆ ☆

Vegan ☐   Gluten Free ☐   Low FODMAP ☐

Vegetarian ☐   Diary Free ☐   Low Carb ☐

Ingredients

_____

_____

_____

_____

_____

_____

Additional Notes

_____

_____

_____

_____

Method

Recipe _____

Source _____

Serves _____ Prep time _____ Cook time _____

My Rating ☆ ☆ ☆ ☆ ☆

Difficulty ☆ ☆ ☆ ☆ ☆

Vegan ☐   Gluten Free ☐   Low FODMAP ☐

Vegetarian ☐   Diary Free ☐   Low Carb ☐

Ingredients

_____

_____

_____

_____

_____

_____

Additional Notes

_____

_____

_____

_____

Method

Recipe _____

Source _____

Serves _____   Prep time _____   Cook time _____

My Rating ☆ ☆ ☆ ☆ ☆

Difficulty ☆ ☆ ☆ ☆ ☆

Vegan ☐   Gluten Free ☐   Low FODMAP ☐

Vegetarian ☐   Diary Free ☐   Low Carb ☐

Ingredients

_____

_____

_____

_____

_____

_____

Additional Notes

_____

_____

_____

_____

_____

Method

Recipe

Source

Serves   Prep time   Cook time

My Rating   ☆ ☆ ☆ ☆ ☆

Difficulty   ☆ ☆ ☆ ☆ ☆

Vegan ☐   Gluten Free ☐   Low FODMAP ☐

Vegetarian ☐   Diary Free ☐   Low Carb ☐

Ingredients

Additional Notes

Method

Recipe _____

Source _____

Serves _____ Prep time _____ Cook time _____

My Rating ☆ ☆ ☆ ☆ ☆

Difficulty ☆ ☆ ☆ ☆ ☆

Vegan ☐   Gluten Free ☐   Low FODMAP ☐

Vegetarian ☐   Diary Free ☐   Low Carb ☐

Ingredients

_____

_____

_____

_____

_____

_____

Additional Notes

_____

_____

_____

_____

_____

Method

Recipe

Source

Serves   Prep time   Cook time

My Rating   ☆   ☆   ☆   ☆   ☆

Difficulty   ☆   ☆   ☆   ☆   ☆

Vegan ☐   Gluten Free ☐   Low FODMAP ☐

Vegetarian ☐   Diary Free ☐   Low Carb ☐

Ingredients

Additional Notes

Method

Recipe _____

Source _____

Serves _____ Prep time _____ Cook time _____

My Rating ☆ ☆ ☆ ☆ ☆

Difficulty ☆ ☆ ☆ ☆ ☆

Vegan ☐ Gluten Free ☐ Low FODMAP ☐

Vegetarian ☐ Diary Free ☐ Low Carb ☐

Ingredients

_____

_____

_____

_____

_____

_____

Additional Notes

_____

_____

_____

_____

Method

Recipe _____

Source _____

Serves _____   Prep time _____   Cook time _____

My Rating   ☆ ☆ ☆ ☆ ☆

Difficulty   ☆ ☆ ☆ ☆ ☆

Vegan ☐   Gluten Free ☐   Low FODMAP ☐

Vegetarian ☐   Diary Free ☐   Low Carb ☐

Ingredients

_____

_____

_____

_____

_____

_____

Additional Notes

_____

_____

_____

_____

_____

Method

Recipe _____

Source _____

Serves _____   Prep time _____   Cook time _____

My Rating   ☆ ☆ ☆ ☆ ☆

Difficulty ☆ ☆ ☆ ☆ ☆

Vegan ☐   Gluten Free ☐   Low FODMAP ☐

Vegetarian ☐   Diary Free ☐   Low Carb ☐

Ingredients

_____

_____

_____

_____

_____

Additional Notes

_____

_____

_____

_____

Method

Recipe

Source

Serves   Prep time   Cook time

My Rating   ☆   ☆   ☆   ☆   ☆

Difficulty   ☆   ☆   ☆   ☆   ☆

Vegan ☐   Gluten Free ☐   Low FODMAP ☐

Vegetarian ☐   Diary Free ☐   Low Carb ☐

Ingredients

___

___

___

___

___

___

Additional Notes

___

___

___

___

___

Method

Recipe _____

Source _____

Serves _____ Prep time _____ Cook time _____

My Rating ☆ ☆ ☆ ☆ ☆

Difficulty ☆ ☆ ☆ ☆ ☆

Vegan ☐   Gluten Free ☐   Low FODMAP ☐

Vegetarian ☐   Diary Free ☐   Low Carb ☐

Ingredients

_____

_____

_____

_____

_____

_____

Additional Notes

_____

_____

_____

_____

Method

Recipe

Source

Serves Prep time Cook time

My Rating ☆ ☆ ☆ ☆ ☆

Difficulty ☆ ☆ ☆ ☆ ☆

Vegan ☐ Gluten Free ☐ Low FODMAP ☐

Vegetarian ☐ Diary Free ☐ Low Carb ☐

Ingredients

_____

_____

_____

_____

_____

_____

Additional Notes

_____

_____

_____

_____

_____

Method

Recipe

Source

Serves   Prep time   Cook time

My Rating   ☆   ☆   ☆   ☆   ☆

Difficulty   ☆   ☆   ☆   ☆   ☆

Vegan ☐   Gluten Free ☐   Low FODMAP ☐

Vegetarian ☐   Diary Free ☐   Low Carb ☐

Ingredients

Additional Notes

Method

Recipe _____

Source _____

Serves _____ Prep time _____ Cook time _____

My Rating ☆ ☆ ☆ ☆ ☆

Difficulty ☆ ☆ ☆ ☆ ☆

Vegan ☐   Gluten Free ☐   Low FODMAP ☐

Vegetarian ☐   Diary Free ☐   Low Carb ☐

Ingredients

_____

_____

_____

_____

_____

_____

_____

Additional Notes

_____

_____

_____

_____

_____

Method

Recipe _____

Source _____

Serves _____ Prep time _____ Cook time _____

My Rating ☆ ☆ ☆ ☆ ☆

Difficulty ☆ ☆ ☆ ☆ ☆

Vegan ☐   Gluten Free ☐   Low FODMAP ☐

Vegetarian ☐   Diary Free ☐   Low Carb ☐

Ingredients

_____
_____
_____
_____
_____
_____
_____

Additional Notes

_____
_____
_____
_____

Method

Recipe _____

Source _____

Serves _____ Prep time _____ Cook time _____

My Rating ☆ ☆ ☆ ☆ ☆

Difficulty ☆ ☆ ☆ ☆ ☆

Vegan ☐   Gluten Free ☐   Low FODMAP ☐

Vegetarian ☐   Diary Free ☐   Low Carb ☐

Ingredients

_____

_____

_____

_____

_____

_____

Additional Notes

_____

_____

_____

_____

Method

Recipe _____

Source _____

Serves _____   Prep time _____   Cook time _____

My Rating   ☆ ☆ ☆ ☆ ☆

Difficulty   ☆ ☆ ☆ ☆ ☆

Vegan ☐   Gluten Free ☐   Low FODMAP ☐

Vegetarian ☐   Diary Free ☐   Low Carb ☐

Ingredients

_____
_____
_____
_____
_____
_____
_____

Additional Notes

_____
_____
_____
_____
_____

Method

Recipe _____

Source _____

Serves _____ Prep time _____ Cook time _____

My Rating ☆ ☆ ☆ ☆ ☆

Difficulty ☆ ☆ ☆ ☆ ☆

Vegan ☐   Gluten Free ☐   Low FODMAP ☐

Vegetarian ☐   Diary Free ☐   Low Carb ☐

Ingredients

_____
_____
_____
_____
_____
_____

Additional Notes

_____
_____
_____
_____

Method

Recipe _____

Source _____

Serves _____ Prep time _____ Cook time _____

My Rating ☆ ☆ ☆ ☆ ☆

Difficulty ☆ ☆ ☆ ☆ ☆

Vegan ☐ Gluten Free ☐ Low FODMAP ☐

Vegetarian ☐ Diary Free ☐ Low Carb ☐

Ingredients

_____
_____
_____
_____
_____
_____

Additional Notes

_____
_____
_____
_____

Method

Recipe _____

Source _____

Serves _____   Prep time _____   Cook time _____

My Rating ☆ ☆ ☆ ☆ ☆

Difficulty ☆ ☆ ☆ ☆ ☆

Vegan ☐   Gluten Free ☐   Low FODMAP ☐

Vegetarian ☐   Diary Free ☐   Low Carb ☐

Ingredients
_____
_____
_____
_____
_____
_____

Additional Notes
_____
_____
_____
_____
_____

Method

Recipe

Source

Serves   Prep time   Cook time

My Rating   ☆ ☆ ☆ ☆ ☆

Difficulty   ☆ ☆ ☆ ☆ ☆

Vegan ☐   Gluten Free ☐   Low FODMAP ☐

Vegetarian ☐   Diary Free ☐   Low Carb ☐

Ingredients

Additional Notes

Method

Recipe _____

Source _____

Serves _____ Prep time _____ Cook time _____

My Rating ☆ ☆ ☆ ☆ ☆

Difficulty ☆ ☆ ☆ ☆ ☆

Vegan ☐   Gluten Free ☐   Low FODMAP ☐

Vegetarian ☐   Diary Free ☐   Low Carb ☐

Ingredients

_____

_____

_____

_____

_____

_____

Additional Notes

_____

_____

_____

_____

Method

Recipe

Source

Serves   Prep time   Cook time

My Rating   ☆ ☆ ☆   ☆ ☆

Difficulty   ☆ ☆ ☆   ☆ ☆

Vegan ☐   Gluten Free ☐   Low FODMAP ☐

Vegetarian ☐   Diary Free ☐   Low Carb ☐

Ingredients

Additional Notes

Method

Recipe

Source

Serves   Prep time   Cook time

My Rating   ☆   ☆   ☆   ☆   ☆

Difficulty   ☆   ☆   ☆   ☆   ☆

Vegan ☐   Gluten Free ☐   Low FODMAP ☐

Vegetarian ☐   Diary Free ☐   Low Carb ☐

Ingredients

Additional Notes

Method

Recipe _____

Source _____

Serves _____ Prep time _____ Cook time _____

My Rating ☆ ☆ ☆ ☆ ☆

Difficulty ☆ ☆ ☆ ☆ ☆

Vegan ☐　　　　Gluten Free ☐　　　　Low FODMAP ☐

Vegetarian ☐　　Diary Free ☐　　　　Low Carb ☐

Ingredients

_____

_____

_____

_____

_____

_____

Additional Notes

_____

_____

_____

_____

Method

Recipe _____

Source _____

Serves _____ Prep time _____ Cook time _____

My Rating ☆ ☆ ☆ ☆ ☆

Difficulty ☆ ☆ ☆ ☆ ☆

Vegan ☐   Gluten Free ☐   Low FODMAP ☐

Vegetarian ☐   Diary Free ☐   Low Carb ☐

Ingredients

_____

_____

_____

_____

_____

_____

Additional Notes

_____

_____

_____

_____

Method

Recipe

Source

Serves   Prep time   Cook time

My Rating   ☆ ☆ ☆   ☆ ☆

Difficulty   ☆ ☆ ☆   ☆ ☆

Vegan ☐   Gluten Free ☐   Low FODMAP ☐

Vegetarian ☐   Diary Free ☐   Low Carb ☐

Ingredients

Additional Notes

Method

Recipe

Source

Serves   Prep time   Cook time

My Rating   ☆   ☆   ☆   ☆   ☆

Difficulty   ☆   ☆   ☆   ☆   ☆

Vegan ☐   Gluten Free ☐   Low FODMAP ☐

Vegetarian ☐   Diary Free ☐   Low Carb ☐

Ingredients

Additional Notes

Method

Recipe _____

Source _____

Serves _____   Prep time _____   Cook time _____

My Rating ☆ ☆ ☆ ☆ ☆

Difficulty ☆ ☆ ☆ ☆ ☆

Vegan ☐   Gluten Free ☐   Low FODMAP ☐

Vegetarian ☐   Diary Free ☐   Low Carb ☐

Ingredients

_____
_____
_____
_____
_____
_____
_____

Additional Notes

_____
_____
_____
_____

Method

Recipe

Source

Serves   Prep time   Cook time

My Rating   ☆   ☆   ☆   ☆   ☆

Difficulty   ☆   ☆   ☆   ☆   ☆

Vegan ☐   Gluten Free ☐   Low FODMAP ☐

Vegetarian ☐   Diary Free ☐   Low Carb ☐

Ingredients

Additional Notes

Method

Recipe _____

Source _____

Serves _____ Prep time _____ Cook time _____

My Rating ☆ ☆ ☆ ☆ ☆

Difficulty ☆ ☆ ☆ ☆ ☆

Vegan ☐ Gluten Free ☐ Low FODMAP ☐

Vegetarian ☐ Diary Free ☐ Low Carb ☐

Ingredients

_____
_____
_____
_____
_____
_____

Additional Notes

_____
_____
_____
_____

Method

Recipe

Source

Serves   Prep time   Cook time

My Rating   ☆   ☆   ☆   ☆   ☆

Difficulty   ☆   ☆   ☆   ☆   ☆

Vegan ☐   Gluten Free ☐   Low FODMAP ☐

Vegetarian ☐   Diary Free ☐   Low Carb ☐

Ingredients

Additional Notes

Method

Made in United States
North Haven, CT
05 December 2021